MAN Up!

A Guide to Restoring Biblical Manhood

MAN Up!

A Guide to Restoring Biblical Manhood

✝

MIKE WINTER

TABLE OF CONTENTS

Introduction ... *vii*

1 Defining a Biblical Man ... 1

2 Loving God and Doing His Will ... 7

Denying Self • The Will of God • A Manly Example

3 Accepting Responsibility ... 31

Priest • Provider • Protector • A Manly Example

4 Connecting to the Family of God ... 67

Worshipping with Believers • Encouraging Believers • Serving with Believers • A Manly Example

5 What's Next? ... 87

Introduction

King David's final words to his son Solomon begin with, "Be strong and be a man!" (1 Kings 2:2, NABRE) David promises Solomon that if he lives this way, his family will never lack a man to sit upon Israel's throne.

I don't have a throne, but I want my children, grandchildren, and every subsequent generation in my family to live forever with me in the Kingdom of God. How will that occur? It will only happen if my sons and their sons live as godly men, real men, and my daughters and their daughters marry such men. What does it mean to be a biblical man? That is what I resolved to discover through God's word and then teach my sons and daughters. The purpose of *Man Up!* is to answer that important question, using the wisdom and principles I discovered in my reading of the Bible.

God loves men. When He created humanity, God started first with a man. When God came to earth to become one of us, He came as a man. A love and appreciation of manhood—its virtue, nobility, and value—is sorely lacking in today's world. The modern view that men are not even necessary for rearing children is unprecedented in world history. In this book, I hope to underscore the value of men and outline the necessity for men to live as godly men.

America is in crisis. So is the rest of the world. The problem? Rudderless living, no consensus on what's right or wrong, the abandonment of biblical values, and the neglect of teaching those values to our children—who therefore grow up depressed, angry, and purposeless because they don't know where they came from, why they are here, or where they are going. Biblical values used to be taught to our children by parents, grandparents, and the church, then reinforced or at least tolerated in academia, media, and government. But in today's world of no absolute truths and "you do you" living, morality is obsolete and the meaning of life elusive, with chaos filling the vacuum.

Exacerbating this problem is the increased absence of fathers present and able to teach their children the word of God so they can walk in the ways of God, which is necessary for a society to thrive. When God gave Eve to Adam, He did so to work through man to create His eternal Kingdom. One man and one woman—joined by God in the covenant of marriage, obedient to His command to be fruitful and multiply and raise godly children—would co-create all the people who would ever live, including those people destined to live forever with God in heaven where He reigns as King and Lord over all. This allegiance to God would be reflected in living rightly before God by loving one another as we love ourselves.

This was and is God's plan for humanity. But too many modern-day Adams have lost their commitment to God and thus have abandoned their responsibility as spiritual leaders of their homes. I believe this is why our homes, churches, and nations are all in such a mess. Too often, men are not godly and men are not leading. This was the problem I sought to address with my sons and daughters when I outlined, based on Scripture, a picture of a biblical man that I and my children could use as a guideline. I and my sons needed to live up to God's vision for manhood. My daughters needed to find men who did the same. Defining for me and my family what a man should be was an important task to complete if I wanted to stand before God as someone faithful to do the work He assigned me as the leader of my home.

Man Up! addresses the need for Christian men and boys to understand what it means to be a man. Too many fathers live without their own or anyone else's definition of a man. Instead, they just do their best to "be good." God created men for more than that. He created men to be real men. Today, fathers with no definition of manhood raise sons with no explanation of manhood. This book attempts to give both fathers and sons a biblical definition of manhood so that fathers can make sure they are living as real men and can train their sons to do the same. Sons who are untrained and don't have a father to train them (whether because of absence or neglect) can use *Man Up!* to learn on their own what it means to be a biblical man.

I have six sons. Sandwiched between my first three sons and my last three are four girls. With my girls, I thought it was vital for them to know what a Christian man is, so that before they "fell in love" they would have an intellectual understanding of what they should be looking for in a husband. Defining a biblical standard of manhood would allow me to remind them of what they should be looking for if they brought a young man home who didn't measure up.

Since marrying off my first three boys and formally recognizing them as men, I have now moved on to preparing my daughters for marriage. The first two boys two of my girls brought to me as potential husbands had never had anyone define a Christian man for them. It has been helpful to them and comforting to me to engage them in the study you are now holding in your hands, so that we were all on the same page when we talked about the expectations of what a Christian man should be.

Sadly, neither of these two young men had a father who taught them about manhood. The first did have a good father, but unfortunately he passed away when his son was only 13. This left a young man to figure out on his own what true manhood was. The man his mother married the second time was not helpful in his journey, but instead caused him to leave home right after high school. The second young man experienced an ugly divorce in his household, creating great alienation between him and his father while he was only a teenager. He fled from his hometown after high school, and he's been trying to figure out biblical manhood on his own since then. Both of these young men came from Christian homes but had never had anyone define for them, as this book will do, what a biblical man is.

I still have three more sons and two more daughters to marry off. I have begun to discuss with them what a Christian man is, using the principles in this study. For the fathers reading *Man Up!*, I hope you will find it helpful as you too raise your sons and teach your daughters what a Christian man should be.

Acknowledgments

Obviously, the first Person I must acknowledge and give credit to for helping me write this book is God. He, in His grace and mercy, took me, a sinner, and saved me before I even knew Him, then set a path before me to experience His abundant plan for my life. He gave me a wife who would become instrumental in giving me a vision to disciple my sons and daughters. He would even place within her heart, then change mine to come into agreement with hers, a desire for God to provide us with ten children for bringing into His Kingdom. Finally, He has saved my children. My sons and daughters are all seeking and serving Jesus despite having a dad who was far from the model Jesus called him to follow. Nevertheless, by His Spirit, the Father has led all of my children to His Son, Whom they are all worshipping today.

Next, I need to thank Pastor Ron Burns for challenging me many years ago to set a biblical target for my first three boys, the only children I had back then. His encouragement for me to put together a ten-week course on biblical manhood for the men of our church was the impetus for what has become this book. I have been using that original study since 2002 for teaching several manhood courses at my church, and have only now written out the answers to the questions I have always used in those courses to lead men and boys to biblical manhood.

I would like to thank my friend Jim Purvis for editing this book. His fingerprints are all over it. It is better because he is a professional extraordinaire in his work, a lover of Jesus and me. Jim is my greatest encourager apart from my wife, and loves me far more than I deserve. His talent is my treasure, with all of us benefiting who read *Man Up!*

My friend Mike Smock was the first to read my edited manuscript, and he immediately committed to helping me publish this tome. His wisdom, encouragement, and assistance helped make this book possible. Mike is a gift from God. He was appointed for such a time as this in my life.

I also want to thank my famous-author friend Todd Wilson, a great family man, who encouraged me to include personal-application stories in the book. The first draft lacked this material. Todd truly blessed me by reading my manuscript and making a great and helpful suggestion.

I mentioned my wife earlier but would like to do so again. I regret to admit that Kim led me (rather than the other way around) into having multiple children and discipling them with intentionality and purpose rather than being just a "good Christian dad." Her encouragement for me to man up was real, and I am so thankful I accepted the challenge. I would not be the man I am today without the woman God placed in my life as His perfect choice for a helpmate.

Finally, I want to thank my children for giving credibility to the words in this book, because they are all Christ-followers and are all great people. Unfortunately, there is no magic formula for raising godly kids. There is no guarantee in the Bible that our children will follow Jesus even when we as parents do everything "right." When it happens, however, despite our sinfulness (and mine is much), there's nothing to be done but praise God for His kindness, and thank Him for giving our children the wisdom and the eyes to see Him clearly so that they can make the best and most important choice of all—to follow Jesus as Savior and Lord. Hallelujah!

Chapter 1

Defining a Biblical Man

I began my study of manhood by thinking about what a man should be. Then, because I am a Christian, I wanted to define not just what a man should be but more specifically what a Christian man should be. The obvious answer? A Christian man should look like Jesus. While for Christians the answer is always Jesus, that answer is not always easily understood or practical. Jesus is a difficult target, due to His deity and perfection. That being said, Jesus will certainly exemplify the manhood definition outlined in this book, and I will include some passages demonstrating what He might have looked like when He lived as a man on the earth. My goal for this book is to give you a helpful tool for measuring yourself as a man, a standard for your sons to aim at, and a test for your future son(s)-in-law to pass.

The opposite of the biblical man is the effeminate man. The effeminate man cannot enter the Kingdom of God (1 Corinthians 6:9). This verse should terrorize the Church today, since it appears the goal of raising boys in the twenty-first century is to make them effeminate.

The Greek word for effeminate in 1 Corinthians meant "soft" and was used to describe boys that men abused sexually. Homosexuality is running rampant in our culture today. Might this be the result of our culture's current proclivity to produce effeminate men?

When I grew up, a man was defined as a conqueror. He conquered women and he conquered other men. At least, that used to be the definition back in the John Wayne days. The modern description of a good man feminizes him so much that he has become almost indistinguishable from a good woman. There's certainly nothing wrong with being strong like John Wayne or sensitive like the new ideal man is encouraged to be. But neither of those extremes is biblical manhood.

I can't entirely blame America's young men for being confused about manhood. First, it's a sad fact that a large percentage of young men today are raised by women. A woman can only raise a boy to be a woman; she isn't equipped to raise a boy to be a man. For a single mother to grow a man, she needs help. That's the role of her extended family and the Church, but, tragically, she rarely, if ever, receives the kind of help she needs. Furthermore, there's now a woke worldview that doesn't believe men are necessary for raising children. This worldview has even invaded many churches. But this is not God's view of how to raise children. All children need a father as well as a mother, because they both serve as important examples and bring significant, unique gifts into a child's life.

Second, except for a brief window of time right after 9/11, when the heroics on that day of the mostly male first responders could not be denied, popular culture has devalued masculinity over the last 50 years. Most men born after 1970 are extremely passive. Why? Because these men have been told all their lives by the culture that masculinity is bad. Even if they have fathers in their homes, boys today often aspire to become like women, because women and their virtues are celebrated in our society. They dress like women and act like women because the culture says women are the better species.

Passivity is nothing new to men. Adam exhibited immense passivity in the Garden, even willing to allow his wife to die in front of him as she ate the forbidden fruit. But passivity is the enemy of manhood. Jesus was never passive. He was always a man with a purpose, and He knew what that purpose was, notably as it tied into His identity as the Son of Man. Jesus never allowed Himself to be shaped by the opinions or desires of the people around Him.

Men today seem to want their wives happy above all else, and think the only way to keep them happy is to avoid conflict with them. This perspective comes from a distorted view of what it means to love our wives like Jesus loves the Church. And this perspective encourages men to be passive. While those in the Church indulge in all sorts of disobedience today, that doesn't mean the Lord is happy about it or approving of it. He will hold accountable everyone who has failed to live according to His commands clearly defined in the Scriptures.

Men are supposed to be the leaders of their homes. Leaders will always experience conflict, because it is not natural for sinful, prideful humans to follow willingly. But a godly man can instill in those he loves a willingness to follow, particularly in his wife, if he loves and serves his family humbly with a clearly defined purpose and direction. It's not that women can't or shouldn't ever lead. It's just that they should lead not in whole but in part. God has made men ultimately responsible for leadership in their families, in their churches, and in society. Where there is responsibility, there is accountability. That is why God went to Adam first, not Eve, after Eve sinned. Adam was responsible for the Garden; therefore, he was held accountable for what happened in the Garden. Sin occurred in the Garden on his watch, in his presence, because of his passivity.

If you will hang in there with me throughout this book, I will demonstrate the biblical truth that men are to be the leaders of their homes and society. This doesn't mean men lead with a fist, but it also doesn't mean they lead from behind rather than in front. God is the most powerful Being in the universe, yet He is also the meekest and gentlest in the universe. Repeatedly, the Bible teaches and models that the Most Powerful serves the weakest. The greatest of all is the servant of all (Matthew 20:26). Men lead by serving, but they are not always leading when they are serving.

God is not passive; He is active. He created the universe and all it contains. He so loved the world that He came to the world to save the world. While presently He allows the world to rebel against Him, ultimately He will judge the world and reward those who love Him and condemn those who reject Him. God initiates salvation by His Spirit, awakening the dead so they can hear the Word of life. God is always working, but He is subtle, quiet, and gentle. Yet He is also strong, vibrant, and consistent.

In the remaining chapters of this book, I will take us through a study of what God has shown us to be His definition of a man. He has displayed this definition in person, and He has commanded this definition from the Scriptures. According to God, a biblical man:

- **M**akes loving God and doing His will first priority
- **A**ccepts responsibility for himself and his family as priest, provider, and protector
- **N**ever is alone, but integrally connects himself to the family of God

Any definition of biblical manhood must begin with loving God and doing His will as the first priority. It is God's first commandment, and therefore reflects the main purpose for which we were created. This book is needed in part because we as men often don't understand what it means to put our minds and hearts into loving God most, loving Him first, and doing His will. I hope to clarify these priorities in the next chapter.

Chapter 2

Loving God and Doing His Will

M—*A biblical man* ***makes*** *loving God and doing His will first priority.*

God in Jesus was clear about what loving God means when He said that if you love Me, you'll obey My commands (John 14:21). Loving God without obeying God is merely pretending to love God. But before we can follow His commands, we must know His commands.

Jesus said our highest good, our first priority, must be to love the Lord our God with all of our heart, soul, mind, and strength. This is the first and greatest commandment (Matthew 22:7). Loving God with all of our minds means pursuing the knowledge of God diligently, fervently, passionately, and consistently through reading and studying the Scriptures.

Unfortunately, many men seem to struggle with reading. However, the tools available to us today for learning God's word are too numerous to make excuses for our ignorance. There are many CDs, DVDs, podcasts, cellphone apps, and so on that provide ways for men to listen to the word of God being read aloud and analyzed. What is sorely lacking in many Christian men today is the willingness to push through their discomfort with reading and consistently set aside time to read the Bible or at least listen to God's word.

Faith comes by hearing God's word, as Paul says in Romans 10:17. If our faith is to grow, we must be in the word of God, because that is where our faith is defined and nourished. It is the word of God where the commands of God are given to us, which will ultimately require faith from us to obey. The key to successfully engaging the Scriptures is for men to create a plan to do so. Men are planners and strategic thinkers; therefore, putting together a consistent means for daily Bible engagement is something men can and must do.

I have found the easiest way to accomplish this mission is to use an annual Bible reading plan and block the first part of my morning for a daily scheduled time to read through the plan. There are many annual Bible-reading plans online. (For example, at my website, knowgodcoach.com, I have a free reading plan you can download.) It's just a matter of choosing a plan you like and then blocking the time to read through the plan.

Those men who aren't good readers or refuse to read can still choose a Bible reading plan from a Bible app and listen to it on their daily commute. Listening to the word of God is less effective than reading it, but it's better than ignoring the word of God. Listening to the Bible while driving will be consumed by the brain but to a lesser extent than reading the Scriptures in a quiet place where you can fully concentrate on what God is saying to you through His word.

The man of God who desires to love God first and most must pursue God first and most. There's no better method for knowing God than spending time in the Scriptures. The Bible is God's provision for us to know Him and learn what He requires from us. Jesus Himself modeled the importance of being a man of the word; He quoted the Scriptures constantly. It's difficult to compare ourselves with Jesus, since He is God, but He came to us as a man so that He could provide an example for us to follow, and He commands us to walk as He did (1 John 2:6).

In Luke 4 we see Jesus being a man of the word in His battle with Satan. Every time Jesus was tempted, He quoted Scripture as His weapon for overcoming temptation. Obviously, that meant Jesus had studied the Scriptures closely and loved them enough to memorize them. You and I must do the same. We must know God's word integrally to resist temptation consistently. Truly, the battle for righteousness is in our hearts and minds before righteousness can show up in our deeds.

Since obedience to God is tied to loving God, we must know the will of God. Again, Paul rebukes the man who refuses to study the Scriptures because that man is ignorant of the word and so is incapable of consistently following God's will. In Ephesians 5:17 (NIV), Paul writes, “Therefore do not be foolish, but understand what the Lord's will is.” There is no better place to discover and understand the Lord's will than the Bible.

The difference between a man and a man of God is time in God’s word and the personal application of His word. Men who ignore Scripture think they are good because they are nice, nonconfrontational, and provide sufficiently for their families. They may even attend church regularly. While some of these generally good behaviors may have a scriptural basis, the clear and specific commands of God's will for men are in the Scriptures. The man of God who is in the word of God is more connected to those commands and is most fully doing those commands. The man ignorant of the word of God often defines his "goodness" by failure to commit "major sins" that the Bible condemns. God doesn't define goodness by failing to do wrong; He defines goodness by obedience to His directives. The man of God who is in the word of God is active in the will of God, whereas the man who is lazy toward the word of God is passive in the will of God. There are few things more damaging to families, churches, and the world than passive men.

It is the word of God revealing to us the will of God that we are to use to spur one another on toward love and good deeds (Hebrews 10:24). Again, the goal is obedience to God, demonstrating our love for God to the world. Therefore. we are not passive in the doing of God's word, nor passive in the pursuit of God through His word. All of the commands found in God's word were perfectly obeyed by Jesus the Savior. All of the commands of God are to be learned and perfect obedience pursued by those whom Jesus saves.

That being said, men are not saved by obeying God's commands. That is a very good thing, because it is impossible for us as sinful men to perfectly obey God. Jesus obeyed all of the Father's commands perfectly so that He could be the perfect sacrifice for all of mankind's sins. His perfect obedience is appropriated to us as our righteousness when we have repented and received Jesus as our Savior. However, as we stated at the beginning of the chapter, obedience to God's word is how we reflect our love for God and express our thankfulness for the work He accomplished for us. As we already saw in John 14:21, Jesus said that those who accept His commandments and obey them are the ones who love Him. So, while obedience does not save us, it demonstrates to God (and men) that we are indeed saved followers of Jesus. We can learn more about what this looks like practically in the next section.

Denying Self

A man loves God by denying himself. Jesus said if anyone would come after Me, he must deny himself, take up his cross, and follow Me (Luke 9:23). He also said that no greater love has any man than this, that he lay down his life for his friends.

As God came into the world denying Himself to save us who are sinners, so men must deny themselves to do the will of God and save sinners. Loving both God and man requires men to die to themselves. This is true in our marriages. It's true in our fathering. It's true in our businesses. It's true in our churches. And it's true in our relationship with God. It's true because it's how God chose to live in the world and requires us as His followers to live in the world.

Everyone thinks about the grandeur of God, the greatness of God, the power of God, and the awesomeness of God. Yet He lives among us, watching and weighing us, to one day reward us or destroy before us the evil works we invested so much time and energy accumulating. We are not free to do whatever we please. Men do all kinds of wickedness before Him who judges all men, because it appears in the temporary that we are getting away with it. For too many men, God seems asleep, ignorant, or disinterested in our evil behavior. Nothing could be further from the truth.

God allows men to do as they please because, in His love, He waits for men to want to please Him. It is His kindness that leads us to repentance (Romans 2:4). He is patient with our sin, returning kindness for evil while Jesus Himself intercedes for us, reminding the Father of His sacrifice on the cross. You and I must sacrifice our self-interest, selfishness, and self-centered ways if we desire to put God's will in place of our own. As husbands and fathers, we get plenty of opportunities to practice self-denial each day in marriage and parenting.

It wasn't just the Lord Jesus who lived a surrendered life, stating that He did not come to do His own will but the will of Him Who sent Him. The Apostle Paul likewise lived a life laid down. In Galatians 2:20 (NIV), Paul says, "I have been crucified with Christ and I no longer live, but Christ lives in me. The life I now live in the body, I live by faith in the Son of God, who loved me and gave Himself for me." Paul consistently demonstrated and constantly taught that the Christian life is a life of service and self-denial, even to physical death.

A practical demonstration of this self-denying life is when we are able to forgive others to the degree that we ourselves want to be forgiven by God. No matter how people wrong us, we must forgive them. Consistently and persistently forgiving our wives and children requires us to deny our flesh and its desire to retaliate and get revenge. Revenge and retaliation are the antitheses of a sacrificial life.

Our efforts to love our wives and children well are God's practical means for teaching us to deny ourselves; our homes are where we as biblical men will most often sacrifice ourselves. We must not choose our careers and the accolades of success over time spent building relationships with our wives and children. We must not choose golf or other hobbies that bring us pleasure over time with our families. It takes discipline and self-denial to make nurturing our family our top priority rather than ourselves and what we often desire to do instead.

Denying ourselves also means not always seeking comfort. One of the most important spiritual missions fathers have is to train their children in the way they should go. This means teaching them God's ways through our example and sharing scriptural truths. Many men are uncomfortable with teaching. However, this is not optional for us as fathers and husbands. Most wives want their husbands to engage them spiritually by sharing the lessons they learn from the Scriptures.

Paul says it's noble for a man to seek church leadership. One of the requirements for being a leader in the church is teaching. Coupled with this requirement is the necessity for a man to lead his home well. While we may not aspire to be leaders in our churches, we must master Scripture to show ourselves workmen who correctly handle the word of truth by teaching it clearly and diligently to our children (2 Timothy 2:15). This doesn't have to be any more complicated than spending our own time in the Bible in the morning, then in the evening sharing with our children what we discovered. Actually, that simple approach is not a bad model to follow. Learn every morning what God has for you in His word for the day, then explain to your family in the evening how you lived that out throughout the day.

Since denying ourselves involves learning how to be the spiritual leader in our home, we must not allow our flesh or the devil to discourage us about our capabilities in this area. We are commanded by God to raise godly children. He does not give us a pass on that command if we think we're not good enough. We may think we're poor readers or inadequate teachers, but, because our children are ours, we are still responsible for leading them in God's ways. Actually, because you are their father, you are the perfect teacher for your children. Embrace that by faith, then pursue that vital work regardless of how you feel.

As you can see, self-denial is twofold. Yes, self-denial requires us to refrain from doing things we want to do that keep us from being the man God has called us to be. But self-denial is also doing things we don't want to do just because we are afraid, tired, or uncomfortable doing them. Embracing both forms of self-denial will help make us strong men of God. This is the real fear of the enemy of our soul. The devil knows that our strength in God will change our families, our churches, our marketplaces, and indeed the world as all men become men of God, strengthened by His power and committed to His purposes.

Living It Out: Personal Stories

Attending homeschool conferences helped me immensely to understand my responsibility to disciple my children. One of the constant refrains I heard at these conferences was that my children would interpret God by my Christian example. That terrified me. I am not a particularly good man and I'm certainly not perfect like Jesus. My shortcomings were not an excuse to not follow Jesus or try to live like Him, but I did not want my children to confuse my often all-too-human behavior as a father with Father God's.

The solution I came up with to this dilemma was for my children to spend time with God daily in His word, just as I was doing. I created the following rule in my house: "No Bible, no breakfast." I read the Bible before breakfast, and I required my children to follow my example and read the Bible before they came to the breakfast table. As soon as possible (somewhere between the ages of three and five, depending on the child) I gave each son or daughter a children's Bible so they could begin reading simple Bible stories. As the children grew older and became better readers, they were given real Bibles and a copy of my annual Bible reading plan, so they could read the same chapters each day that I was reading. Receiving a new "adult" Bible on their birthday or at Christmas was a real milestone for my children, a recognition that they had achieved significant maturity in their lives, which caused them to engage in the daily discipline of Bible reading eagerly.

The fruit of this discipline? My children began to recognize Who the One True God really is and what He requires of us. This led to them voluntarily complying with the will of God. It also meant they began to point out my failures in living according to God's word, which caused me to grow spiritually—after I humbled myself before them and before God!

The Will of God

A man loves God by making the will of God his first priority. The perfect man is Jesus. You and I are born again to be just like Jesus. Romans 8:29 says God is on a mission to conform us into the likeness of His firstborn Son. In John 6:38, Jesus states His purpose in coming to earth was not to do His own will but the will of the Father who sent Him. Likewise, the man who loves God makes doing the will of God his highest priority.

This does not mean everyone needs to leave their vocations and become full-time pastors or missionaries. It means that first and foremost, a man's occupation needs to be seeing that God's Kingdom comes to earth as it is in heaven. In our homes, workplaces, and neighborhoods, the ways of God are to be lived out and shared with all those around us, regardless of what we do as our vocation. Stated another way, our *occupation* is what we do for God to advance His Kingdom; our *vocation* funds that work. This distinction is critical for understanding how to become the men God calls us to be.

How do we know what the will of God is? We looked at this question earlier, where we learned we are not to be ignorant of God's will but to know it. The command from God in Ephesians 5:17 would not be given to us were it impossible for us to know His will. How do we know His will? His will is recorded for us in the word of God. Paul reiterates this in Romans 12:2 (ESV) when he writes, "Do not be conformed to this world, but be transformed by the renewal of your mind." We renew our minds by reading the Bible. We must be in the Scriptures consistently so we know what they say, can do what they say, and can teach what they say. We have no other means of knowing God's will than God's word.

While we don't have any photos of Jesus reading the Torah, we know He was an expert in it, because at age 12 He discussed it with the religious leaders and later gave His life to fulfill every word in the Torah that concerned the Messiah. Of course, Jesus' teachings became inspired Scriptures recorded in the New Testament. But many of His instructions were simple explanations of the Father's heart previously recorded in the Old Testament. We also know Jesus valued the Scriptures of His day because, as noted previously, when He battled Satan, His weapon was God's word, which He quoted back to the devil. When the devil spoke God's word to Him, Jesus corrected his use of those Scriptures, clarifying the purpose for which God had recorded them. Jesus is our example of manhood and requires us to be His disciples. That means that we, like Jesus, must be men who clearly and unequivocally know the word of God.

In John 5, Jesus said He did what He saw His Father doing. How do you and I see what the Father is doing? It begins with the Scriptures, but this is where the power of prayer enters the picture. The Holy Spirit has been given to us to clarify for us how we can apply God's word to our lives. As you and I read the Scriptures and God reveals through them His general will for us, our prayers are a means of responding to God's word. We receive His general revelation in the Bible, then we seek Him through prayer to learn the specific application. We see what the Father is doing when we understand what He is saying from the Scriptures. Then we take that understanding and make it real when we live it out before our wives, children, and neighbors.

The importance of doing God's will cannot be overstated. For the most part, men take a passive view toward living lives obedient to God's word. We demonstrate this passivity by our lack of interest in regularly reading and studying the Scriptures. In Matthew 7:21–23, Jesus warns those who fail to do God's will that they will miss the kingdom of heaven. Interestingly, those who miss the kingdom are those who did great works for God before men. Those who complain to Jesus for being condemned by Jesus are those who had healed the sick and performed many miracles, yet God says they did not do His will.

Most of God's will is accomplished in the mundane, not the spectacular. We tend to define obedience as the big things we don't do, like not murdering anyone or not committing adultery. But God also measures obedience in the little things we are supposed to do, like being patient with our wives, speaking kind words to our children, and loving others unconditionally. "Faithful in little, faithful in much," Jesus taught. Not, "You can be faithful in a big thing to compensate for your unfaithfulness in the little things." We get it wrong when we think we must do something spectacular for God or we are of no value. We must be faithful men who consistently obey Him in the minutiae of our daily living among the people He has given us to love and serve. That is how we put His will first in our lives: by loving our neighbor as we love ourselves, thus demonstrating our love for God with all our heart, soul, mind, and strength.

Practical Examples

Here are some critical areas for loving God and doing His will that we as godly men can practically do and measure in our lives. The first area is giving. God so loved the world that He gave (John 3:16). Jesus gave His life so that we could have peace with God. Greater love has no man than this: that a man lay down his life for his friends (John 15:13). Giving is fundamental to God's nature, so it must be to the man of God as well. What does giving look like? In financial terms, most churches would have us commit to giving at least ten percent of our income—that is, a tithe. This should probably be the minimum goal of our giving.

When you try to study tithing in the New Testament, you come up empty. The only time Jesus mentions tithing is when He rebukes the religious leaders for tithing the minuscule things of this world while ignoring God's relational commands for the world. Jesus invites us into a sacrificial lifestyle under the New Covenant. Since Jesus taught that lustful thoughts are the same sin as adultery and harsh words the same as murder, we can extrapolate this principle into all areas of our lives, including giving. It's clear that Jesus demands more from us than a simple legalistic religious adherence to Him (see the Sermon on the Mount in Matthew 5–7).

As men we struggle to give because we are selfish and greedy, and fear we won't have enough for ourselves. Fear is the opposite of faith, which God requires of us to please Him (Hebrews 11:6). Giving generously to our churches to advance God's Kingdom, as well as giving generously to our wives, children, extended families, and neighbors, releases in us the nature of God's extraordinary giving. God gives generously, and so too will the obedient man of God.

After giving, the second critical area for loving God and doing His will is the obedient act of serving. Jesus came not to be served but to serve others by laying down His life for all (Matthew 20:28). The greatest of all is the servant of all (Matthew 23:11). Serving is not the same as giving. Serving is using our time and talents to build God's Kingdom, while giving is using our treasure to build God's Kingdom. Each of us has a place in God's Kingdom, for building it up in breadth and depth until the whole world knows Jesus and lives like Jesus. When we come to Jesus as His sons, we come to Him as His servants, bought by His blood (1 Corinthians 6:20). Serving is the next level after giving to increase our obedience while decreasing our self-centeredness. Serving others so that people everywhere can see and experience Jesus through us is the obedient lifestyle of the follower of Jesus, Who served all as Savior of all.

The third practical and critical area in obeying God's will involves the gospel: the obedient disciple of Jesus shares the gospel with others. The Great Commission is the mission of every Christian. When Jesus began His ministry, He told His disciples His purpose was to make them fishers of men (Mark 1:17). Jesus concluded His ministry by calling the disciples His witnesses who would go into all the world and make other disciples (Matthew 28:19–20). If you and I are disciples of Jesus, we are ambassadors for Christ through whom He is appealing to men to be reconciled to God (2 Corinthians 5:20). This doesn't mean we have to be full-time evangelists. But it does mean we are eager to do the work of evangelism, because we realize that apart from Christ the eternal destiny of all men is hell, but the Good News we possess is God's means for avoiding that horrific eternal destiny. We share the gospel to bring those men who will believe, receive, and obey the gospel message into eternal life with their Savior.

We cannot be ashamed of Jesus and be His disciple (Luke 9:26). We shouldn't be obnoxious about our faith, but we must stop being afraid of identifying with our Lord (1 Peter 3:15). Not only are we responsible for training our children in the faith by teaching them the gospel, but we should also share the gospel with all those God has placed in our sphere of influence. At the end of each year we should ask ourselves, Who did I help enter the Kingdom of God this year? This is why the Church, of which we are a part, has been left on the earth: to bring others into the Kingdom.

Finally, the obedient Christian man has to sacrifice for His Lord. I don't know when, I don't know how, but at some point you will be asked to give more than you're giving now or more than you're comfortable giving of your treasure, time, and talents to seeing God's Kingdom come and His will be done on earth as it is in heaven. Godly men sacrifice for the welfare of others. Not usually unto death, but sometimes even unto death. Sacrifice, from little daily sacrifices to the ultimate sacrifice of dying on the Cross, is what the Man of God did. So it should come as no surprise that sacrifice will be required at various times by the man of God who seeks to follow the Son of God. We are on a journey of transformation into the image of the Firstborn Son (Romans 8:29). Our journey, like His, will require the absolute surrender of our lives. Sometime, somewhere, God will call on you to give your all, even as He calls you to carry your cross daily. Sacrifice is the ultimate surrender to the ways of God for the glory of God, required by God of the obedient man of God.

Jesus obeyed His Father perfectly, so you and I are to aspire to obey God perfectly, too. If we have any lingering doubts about this, God's warning to us in Matthew 7:21–23, mentioned earlier, should put an end to those doubts. In these verses, God warns the religious that failure to obey His will, regardless of their vast amount of spiritual works, will keep them from living with God forever. It is the will of God we must concern ourselves with above all else, which can most easily be found in the word of God. The Holy Spirit then helps us live out God's will in practical ways, as in prayer we seek the Spirit's help for specific direction and application.

A Manly Example

I want to conclude the letter "M" of the man definition with an example of someone who lived out what it means to love God and do His will as first priority. I can think of no better example than Jesus. I realize that Jesus is the best and ultimate answer for every instance of every Biblical principle, but that doesn't mean we should dismiss how Jesus lived out His life on earth as a man. Jesus was completely human, just as you and I are human, except for our sin nature. Because Jesus was born of a virgin, He was not cursed with a sin nature from birth. However, He did have the capacity to sin (Hebrews 4:15). But He chose not to ever sin, so that He could obey the Father perfectly and offer Himself as the perfect sacrifice for the sins of all mankind. This is why Jesus is truly the best example of a biblical man Who loved God most by putting God's will first in His life.

1 John 2:6 states that you and I must walk as Jesus did. This means we must live as Jesus lived. Jesus lived not to do His will but the will of His Father (John 6:38). The will of the Father was His very food, even when He hadn't eaten in 40 days (John 4:34). This commitment to the will of God must become our commitment. Our culture,

our families, and our churches are such a mess because too often we as men lack Jesus' commitment to God's will more than our selfish will. The will of God is clear, though not specific. The will of God is that we love Him with all of our heart, soul, mind, and strength. We have already discussed what this means, but to reemphasize the basics, it at least means that we as men should spend consistent time with God through reading His word and praying, and seek to make Him known as Savior and Lord to the world.

God the Father plans to conform each of us to the image of God the Son. That was His plan for us from the beginning of time (Romans 8:29). We might as well get going on living as Jesus did, for we will certainly do so when we live forever with God and all those who have ever loved Him. Jesus' choice to live perfectly and impute His righteousness to us does not excuse us from our need to try to live perfectly, too. Jesus as much as commanded us to live perfect lives in Mathew 5:48. Our frequent failure at executing this command is not permission to stop trying to obey it. God expects us to love Him most and do His will first. I don't think He will accept our excuses for failure to try when we meet Him face to face.

Jesus said He came to seek and save the lost (Luke 19:10), and develop fishers of men (Mark 1:17). While knowing God comes first in loving God, making God known to the world is how we express our love for God. Jesus spent time with His Father so He could personally know the Father's specific will for Him. His Father's love for us expressed this will in sending Jesus into the world to be our Savior. You and I must spend time with the Father as Jesus did if we are to accomplish the will of the Son, Who commanded us to go and make disciples. "Living like Jesus" means seeking and saving the lost people in our lives while equipping every person in our lives to obey Jesus just as we are doing.

Chapter 3

Accepting Responsibility

> **A**—*A biblical man* ***accepts*** *responsibility for himself and his family as priest, provider, and protector.*

To be a biblical man, you must be a priest, provider, and protector for yourself and your family. But what does this mean in practical terms? We will unpack these concepts in the following sections.

Priest

Our first role as husbands and fathers is to serve our family as priests. Jesus calls us priests in His final visit to the Apostle John, described in Revelation 1:5–6. The function of a priest is to bring God to men and men to God. Our role as husbands and fathers is to pray for our wives and children, bring them to God, and teach our wives and children God's word, therefore bringing God into our home.

We cannot lead our families spiritually if we are not leading ourselves spiritually. The primary complaint of Christian wives is: "My husband doesn't lead us spiritually." Most spiritually impotent husbands would agree that the person in their family who pursues Jesus the most is the wife and mother of the family. This simply should not be.

The word of God has been given to us by God for knowing Him and doing His will. None of us are born with a knowledge of God and an inclination to obey Him; the opposite is true. We are born rebels against God, defiant of God and His control over our lives. The desire to be our own God is most evident in our toddler years but continues throughout our adult years, and is only managed by our daily dying to self through obedience to the lordship of Jesus.

One of my favorite Bible stories is that of God's description of selecting Abraham to be the founder of His chosen people. In Genesis 18:19, God says He chose Abraham because he would obey God's ways and teach them to his children. This is excellent news for us as fathers, because all of us can be like Abraham and choose to obey God's word and teach it to our children. Just as this was the criteria God used for choosing a man when He decided to create the nation of Israel, this is the same criteria God wants to see in you so He can turn your family into a nation of Christ followers. And because you have the Holy Spirit, you are even better equipped to do this than Abraham!

Without leading ourselves spiritually, we cannot fulfill the work of God in our home. But what if we embrace the work of reading the Bible regularly and sharing what we learn with our families consistently? In that case, we will be doing the work of God in our home, following the example of Abraham, and increasing the probability of our children living with us eternally in heaven. I can think of no greater incentive for us as men to be spiritual leaders of ourselves and our loved ones than this.

Teaching the Scriptures to your family is the byproduct of your time alone with God. You must cultivate your own relationship with God first. Then leading your family spiritually from this solid foundation is not as difficult as you might think. Here's my approach: I write a verse from my daily Bible reading in a journal—whatever verse God laid on my heart that day for whatever reason. Then, I write down a few thoughts about that verse. Why did it catch my attention? What is God asking me to do in this verse? What is He revealing about Himself? What principle for godly living can I extract from this verse? At my kitchen table after dinner or in the living room before bed, I pull out my journal and share my verse with the family, along with my thoughts about it. I like to have my children read the verse and maybe a few other verses surrounding it for context before explaining my thoughts to them. If you adopt this practical and simple method, you will be teaching your family God's word and taking your place as God's priest over your home.

Saturating ourselves with God's word so that we know how to resist God's enemy is the secret to being an effective personal and family priest. We must therefore work to know God. He commands us to be workmen who correctly handle the word of truth (2 Timothy 2:15). We begin the work of knowing God by battling our flesh and its natural inertia and choosing to spend time with God through the discipline of daily Bible reading and prayer. No faithful man of God has ever existed who didn't spend regular time with God, listening to His voice and sharing with Him his heart. As we learn about God and His general will for us in the Scriptures, the Holy Spirit helps us discern God’s specific will.

God’s command for us to do our best to show ourselves worthy of His approval, workmen with no need to be ashamed who rightly handle the word of truth, underscores His expectation of us as men, particularly as it applies to being spiritual leaders of our homes. This command from God through Paul is imperative for us to embrace. Are we doing our best to open the Bible and learn it for ourselves? Would we be comfortable standing before God and saying as much? Would He consider us workers at His word, men exerting time, effort, and energy to know the Bible so we can grow spiritually? If not, we need to fix that immediately.

The Holy Spirit uses the Scripture—which is living and active and sharper than any two-edged sword (Hebrews 4:12)—to teach, rebuke, correct, and train us (2 Timothy 3:16) in God's ways so we can live for His glory. The power of the Holy Spirit in our lives directly correlates to our intake of God's word into our lives. Today, the word of God is so easy to access through print, media, and audio that we have no excuse for not partaking daily in God's food for our souls. Without the daily discipline of Scripture intake and meditation, we cannot grow or lead spiritually, either ourselves or others. As I mentioned in the previous chapter, the simplest means I have found for accomplishing consistent Bible reading is to commit to a Bible reading plan. These plans abound online. You can download an app or print a plan out, but having a conveniently available daily plan for Bible reading makes daily reading an easy plan to execute.

We cannot be effective priests without God's help; we cannot be effective priests without strong faith. Faith comes by hearing the word of God (Romans 10:17). We cannot lead in the Spirit without being filled by the Spirit, Whose energy and power in our lives is a direct reflection of His word in our lives. God wants godly children; that is His purpose for marriage (Malachi 2:15). God commands us to instruct our children in the Law (Deuteronomy 6:7), in the wisdom literature (Proverbs 1:8, 4:1, 4:10, 4:20, 5:1, 5:7), and in the New Testament (Ephesians 6:4). God has determined that parents—particularly fathers—are the primary missionaries to the next generation of humanity. You and I are those missionaries if we have children, and we are expected to do our jobs with all diligence. Our children's coming to biblical faith will be primarily influenced by our sharing our own faith with them. Our children's eternal destiny is, in part, riding upon our efforts to train them in God's word. There is no more important reason than that to be men of God's word and effective priests in our homes.

Living It Out: Personal Stories

As priest of my home, I trained my children spiritually in three ways. First, the "no Bible, no breakfast" program concluded every morning with everyone sharing at the breakfast table a verse that had been especially meaningful to them from their Bible reading that day. So in addition to reading their Bible, each child was required to share something from their reading with the family. The youngest children retold in their own words the simple Bible stories they read from their children's Bible; the children old enough to be reading actual Bibles would write their verse of the day in a journal and record their thoughts about it; these journal entries would then be shared around the table. My wife and I also participated in this discipline of recording our verse of the day and our thoughts about it in our journals. This habit continues not only with me and Kim but with our adult children as well.

The second way I spiritually trained my children was through daily devotions after dinner. I began with a simple program called Keys for Kids (www. keysforkids.org) that contained a Bible verse to read, a story about the verse, and a "key for kids" section that summarized the lesson from the reading. Encouraging my children to guess the daily "key for kids" was great fun around our kitchen table. Since my children have aged out of these simple dinner devotions, I now share my particular verse of the day in the evening with my family, while the children still share their verses in the morning with their mother.

The challenge to continuing these traditions comes when the children get older and involve themselves in numerous extracurricular activities. It takes great discipline to keep the family together when so many opportunities exist for everyone to get busy doing their own things. We have tried to limit our children to participating in one sport only during each season of the school year (fall, winter, and spring), and have them all in the same sport so that these busy seasons are more manageable. God's priest in the home has to be highly intentional with his family if he is to be faithful at shepherding them well.

Finally, Wednesday night is family night in our household. Family night activities include singing some worship songs (usually obtained through YouTube), then watching a DVD teaching series on a Christian topic or going through a Christian-themed book for discussion afterward. Kim and I did not and do not send our children to church-sponsored weekly youth activities, choosing instead to train our children ourselves—which I would suggest is more effective at producing godly children.

Even though many of my children are well into adulthood, family night continues in the Winter household, with my married children coming over each Wednesday night to sing and learn along with their younger siblings. (Offering free dinner to these newly married couples is a helpful incentive!) The fact that my older kids still participate in family night reinforces to their brothers and sisters still living at home the importance of our family walking with Jesus by seeking His face together.

Provider

A godly man provides for himself and his family physically, practically, and spiritually. The Bible has some high expectations of men as providers for their homes, and serious consequences for those who fail. God says those who fail to provide for their families are worse than infidels (1 Timothy 5:8). I don't know what is worse than an infidel, but I do know that infidels don't get to heaven but spend eternity in hell. That is a destiny we don't want, and certainly we don't want one worse than that!

Likewise, those who can but don't work are to be ignored by the church (2 Thessalonians 3:10). While most modern churches are too compassionate to obey God in this matter, the Scripture is clear that a church should not feed a man who refuses to work. People holding up signs for money are begging, not working. Work is good for the individual and provides value to society. Supporting the able-bodied beggar encourages laziness and should not be practiced by Christians. God frowns on such laziness when He commands us to avoid living such unproductive lives (Titus 3:14).

God gave Adam work before the Fall, which means work is good and noble, not a punishment (Genesis 2:15). While work results were cursed after the Fall, work itself was not. I plan on being put to work in heaven, where Jesus says cities exist and city managers are leading them (Luke 19:17). Work gives us meaning, purpose, and significance. These things are imperative for healthy living.

There is a lot of confusion today over the idea of men providing for their homes. In the traditional America of yesteryear, men and women had clearer roles. Men worked outside their homes as providers, while women worked within their homes as caretakers. Today men and women work outside the home vocationally for income in nearly equal numbers. The modern view of providing is that both men and women work outside the home to meet the family's needs. But is this a biblical model?

The Bible does not state that men must work outside the home and women must work inside the home. Or, said another way, the Bible does not explicitly say that men must provide all of the financial means for the family, while women attend to the emotional and relational needs. In fact, the Proverbs 31 woman seems to contribute some income to the family. While this appears inarguable, it is probable that she provided a supplemental source of income rather than the primary source. Her husband sat at the city gate; such men were city leaders, chosen because of their wealth (usually because of their property holdings). So even in this instance, the husband was the primary provider.

There are other more direct arguments I can make from the Bible to prove that a man should be the primary provider for his home. The first one is based on Genesis 2:15, where God assigns work to Adam before He created Eve. Eve was created to help Adam with his assignment to care for the Garden, but she was not given the primary responsibility for the Garden. The responsibility to work and keep the Garden was Adam's.

Second, following the Fall, God calls Adam to account first, even though he was not the first to eat the fruit. Indeed, God knew that the serpent and then Eve had helped lead Adam astray, but Adam was ultimately responsible for what went on in the Garden, so, as such, God went to him first to discuss what happened, not Eve.

Third, a man is commanded to leave his parents' home and cleave to his wife (Genesis 2:24). Why is the man responsible for leaving and cleaving and not the woman? The assumption is that the young man and the young woman live under their parents' provision and protection before marriage. The man leaves and cleaves when he can provide a new home for his wife, who will then leave her father's protection and provision and join her husband, who now becomes her provider. This is symbolized in the marriage ceremony by the father of the bride "handing" his daughter over to the groom at the altar. The woman is to stay with her parents until the man she marries can provide for her on his own. The woman's purity is represented by the white wedding dress, having been protected by her father who "kept" her while she lived in his house. I understand that in today's world many women, perhaps all women, can provide for themselves without a man. But historically that's not how it's always been, nor is it God's plan for a married woman.

Most of the Third World still operates according to these principles. While often this is because in these cultures the woman is considered a lesser person (which biblically she is *not*), this traditional way of living in most of the world, much of which is not Christian, further demonstrates the inherent nature of God's plan for men and women to function together before and after marriage.

Fourth, Paul instructs Timothy to teach the young widows to marry, have children, and manage their households (1 Timothy 5:14). The women can stay in their homes and manage them because the responsibility to provide for the homes belongs to their husbands.

Finally, in keeping with his instruction to Timothy, Paul tells Titus to instruct the young women to love their husbands and work at home, presumably in managing the children and attending to the other daily tasks of the household (Titus 2:4–5).

These instructions from Paul to Timothy and Titus are significant because these men are Paul's protégés for taking the gospel to the churches he planted and helping those churches become better established. Therefore, these instructions were not just haphazard orders to two young pastors; they were doctrine for the early Church, and therefore should be considered applicable to families today.

This biblical idea—that men are to work outside the home to provide shelter and provision for their families while women are to work within the home to responsibly care for their families—is offensive to secular culture and even to many within the current generation of Christians. I believe this is because many in the church have wandered far from the faith and the admonition to obey all that Jesus commanded.

Certainly, a woman can work outside the home, especially when necessary. As godly men, however, our goal should be to provide sufficiently for our family's physical needs so that our wives do not have to work. Indeed, if we look to the Bible as our guide, no man should marry until he has a home to bring his wife to, and the income necessary to sustain her and the children that result from the marriage.

All this might sound new and strange to some young readers; that's why many young couples marry too early, before the man can provide for his wife and the couple is ready for children. The primary purpose of marriage is children. This is God's main reason for commanding that two become one flesh, so that they produce godly offspring (Genesis 1:27–28, 3:20; Malachi 2:15). But a young couple should not have children immediately, not until the man's income level is sufficient for the family to survive on his income alone, so his wife can stay home and raise their kids. Regrettably, most couples today do not even consider this path. Instead, they marry and the wife immediately starts working outside the home, because a second income is necessary to make ends meet. In many cases, much of that second income goes to paying for their children's childcare, which means their children are being raised or at least greatly influenced by people other than themselves.

This principle that the man is responsible for the physical provision of his home leads naturally to the practicalities of caring for the family's essential needs. Food, shelter, transportation, rest, organization, and safety are practical necessities that the man of God should provide for his family. Members of our church can help us as husbands and fathers meet our family's needs in whatever area we lack knowledge. Simple car repairs, home repairs, and routine home maintenance are all things we can learn from others by asking for help. (When we learn how to do things as we receive this help, we can then in turn be helpful to others struggling in those same areas.) This is part of what it means to provide for our families practically. In no way can a man afford to be lazy. A man's job is to provide everything his family needs for healthy living. This will look different for each man and family, but the goal is the same for every godly man: his wife and children must feel cared for and provided for.

Another aspect of practical provision is training our children in the basics of running a home. We all as biblical men should have at least some of the required skills, which we can then teach our children. If we lack skills in certain areas, we should invite other trusted men into our homes who can teach us and our children. For example, I am good at managing money and have taught my children money management. However, I am terrible with construction projects; luckily, I have friends who are excellent. My boys have worked with such men and learned much from them, even as they have watched me learn from them and execute work projects around our house.

The most important practical skill we all can teach our children is to have a good work ethic. This is best caught through personal experience rather than taught. When they are old enough, our children should be doing all of the inside and outside maintenance of our homes. Cooking, cleaning, mowing, shoveling, and weeding can be done by our older children;

performing these chores will teach them how to work and at the same time prepare them for home ownership. While we fathers have a labor force under our roof—our children—we should train our labor force. As I tell my children, I started in labor and will end in labor when you are gone, but while you are here, I'm in management, responsible for training you in labor. The poor work ethic of many in the Millennial workforce directly correlates with parenting that ignores this principle of provision.

Finally, a man must provide spiritually. As was discussed earlier, God intends for men to be the spiritual leaders of the home. Leadership doesn't mean men have to know more about the Bible than their wives—though that is certainly a good goal! It means ensuring that the spiritual training and development of your family takes place. It means taking the lead in finding and attending a Bible-believing church. It means initiating discussions about Jesus and His word at home. It means owning the responsibility for bringing your children to saving faith and helping your wife grow in her faith.

That being said, you should not neglect to utilize your wife's knowledge, experience, and wisdom in helping your children come to faith.

Part of being a good leader is empowering others to accomplish what must be done, and that certainly includes partnering with our wives to win our children to Christ. But a good leader does not abrogate his responsibility either. Men, you are responsible for the spiritual temperature of your home. If you are cold to the ways of God and the word of God, don't expect the spiritual fire in your wife to be sufficient for winning your children to Jesus. Ultimately it is your responsibility to provide—by your direct involvement with your children and with the help of others (your wife, Christians within your extended family, pastors, Sunday school teachers, etc.)—the spiritual resources necessary to lead your children to saving faith in Christ.

Living It Out: Personal Stories

A man provides by working to earn income for his family; teaching this critical discipline to my children was not easy. When my three oldest children were young boys, I signed them up for a weekly paper route. They started working at ages seven, nine, and eleven. I included their grandpa in the mix; he took them on their routes after picking up the newspapers, which freed me up to attend to my own work responsibilities! Each boy earned $10 a week. After they had been working for a while I taught them a class on how to manage their money properly. Earning their own money allowed my boys to become providers early; they paid for all of their sports activities, and the accoutrements they desired for looking their best doing those activities. They also had to purchase with their own money the birthday and Christmas gifts they gave to their siblings. Having so many siblings placed significant pressure on their finances, making them hard workers and good stewards of what they earned.

As they grew older, I helped all of my children obtain jobs at local businesses. One of the best jobs they had was working at a local McDonald's from 6:00 A.M. to noon. Because my children were homeschooled, these morning hours were available to them for working. These were the best hours for my children to work in such an establishment, since the often-poor influence of other children is generally not present during these morning hours (children who are not homeschooled usually work in the afternoon). My only negative experience with McDonald's was when my daughters worked there and occasionally a male customer would speak evil things to them. We eventually moved them to Chick-fil-A, where I found the clientele had fewer sexually assaulting words to offer my daughters. To this day, my children still at home all work to provide funding for their sports and family gifts. Right now my 13- and 15-year-olds work at a local church and help people with yard work to earn money.

I should also mention here that I never paid my children an allowance for participating in the routine upkeep of our home. They live here and therefore are required to serve the family by working on various tasks to keep our home thriving. This includes making meals, performing other kitchen duties, and weekly house cleaning. None of the household tasks were assigned by gender; my boys and girls participated in all of the chores (for example, my daughters did yard work, including taking their rotation on the lawn mower).

The only way I know of to train a man to work is to put him to work when he is young. They don't like it, but they learn that work is a normal part of life when trained early to do it. They also grow up outperforming their peers who have been idle their entire lives. As my older boys (and daughters) entered the marketplace, they all excelled there.

Protector

A biblical man protects himself and his family from the flesh and the devil. Being a protector requires moral integrity. 1 John 2:16 describes three areas of the flesh that men must protect themselves and their families from indulging: the lust of the flesh, the lust of the eyes, and the pride of life. When speaking with men I like to refer to these three areas simply as pleasure, possessions, and promotions.

Pleasure

Pleasure and comfort are natural to the flesh, and men must overcome their propensity to want easy gratification—which is the desire to feel good and do nothing. The antidote to this propensity is to do hard things, to create habits that push our abilities and cause us to strain and sweat at something which makes us mentally and physically stronger.

Perhaps the best discipline a man can pursue, after daily Bible reading, is daily exercise. Even the Apostle Paul says it is a good thing (1 Timothy 4:8). I am not talking about using exercise primarily as a means to build muscles or lose weight. As a culture we are too obsessed with body image. As godly men we should see exercise as a form of disciplining our flesh. When we do something strenuous that pushes us mentally and physically, it strengthens us in our battle with sin. So pick an exercise, any exercise, and do it regularly, but do it in a way that gets you faster, stronger, and better because you demand more effort from yourself as you progress. Try to exercise five or six days a week. Again, the purpose is to create self discipline, to remind ourselves that our flesh is not the boss of us but is our servant to do the will of God and complete the work God has assigned us.

The saints of old used fasting to control their flesh. If you refuse to exercise to help tame your flesh, then I encourage you to fast regularly. Once a week is a common fasting goal, but if that's too hard, fast no less than once a month. Denying yourself food helps you take command over your flesh. Nothing screams more adamantly from our flesh than its desire for food. Fasting and exercising helps men gain control mentally and spiritually over their physical desire for comfort and pleasure.

Two lust-of-the-flesh areas men seem to pleasure themselves with regularly are pornography and gaming. Pornography is a means for men to receive the sexual pleasure they are too lazy to obtain from a woman. This is a hard word, but please hear me out. If we are single, we need to become a biblical man, as defined in this book, so we are ready to marry. Once we are marriage eligible (we are pursuing God, have a good job, and have the means to provide a good home for a mate), we need to pray for God's direction and then start meeting women who could potentially become our wife. These women should be godly, want to mother children, and partner with you in ministry. It is beyond the scope of this book to fully define a biblical woman, but these three qualities of a wife should be on your list.

Single men use pornography as a shortcut to pleasuring themselves sexually because they're not doing the hard work of preparing themselves to be a godly man and obtain a godly wife. Sexual self-denial until God provides such a woman is the biblical mandate for single men. Sleeping with women while unmarried is sinful; the Bible refers to this as fornication. Sexual activity within the marriage of a man and a woman is God-ordained and beautiful; all other sexual activity is fornication. Christian men are commanded not to participate in such activity.

For the married man, pornography is the lazy man's way to sexually pleasure himself because he's not in a right relationship with his wife. The woman in the pornographic picture or video is submissive and willing all the time to give herself to the man. This is highly attractive to the husband who is disengaged from his wife. Our wives are not the women portrayed in pornography; they never will be. Pornography is a fantasy, and fantasies are false. They show as real something that is not. As a married man, you quickly discover that your wife is not the same as the women in the porn you've consumed. You must stop pretending that she is, even stop wishing that she would be. Pornography is demeaning for the women who participate in it. They are usually coached by ungodly men to falsely portray how women want to be treated.

Biblically, your sexual command is to please your wife. We are to focus on her needs, pleasures, and desires. You also have to work hard at keeping your overall relationship healthy so that she wants to sleep with you. You have to resolve conflict. You have to speak the truth to her about your desires and needs. You have to "play the man," which involves reconciling, forgiving, and talking through issues. The easy, unmanly, pornographic road leads to selfish, unsatisfying self-pleasure instead of a healthy and pure relationship with your wife. Pornography destroys your relationship with your wife by creating a distance in your heart from her. It puts in your head a false notion of what is true about sex and the nature of a woman. It is the passive man's means to sexual gratification, and it is ungodly, unbiblical, and sinful. Men of God should have nothing to do with it.

Gaming is the other area where many men seek pleasure more than they should. I'm talking about the man sitting alone on the couch for hours playing video games. Gaming is tricky because it's not as sinful as pornography. (Although many video games contain pornographic content. It goes without saying that a biblical man should stay far away from such games.) The type of game, as long as it is not filled with porn or graphic violence, is irrelevant; the issue with gaming is the time it steals from better activities. A man sitting on the couch to escape from the world is not a man busy protecting himself or his family from the world. Our job is to model, especially for our children, how to engage in healthy activities that build community, even when that community is only in our home. Not engaging in these types of activities is a habit we usually fall into as single men before marriage.

All this doesn't mean men should never take time for pleasure. But if we are married, it does mean we should resist pursuing pleasure by ourselves. Our pleasurable activities should include being with members of our family, not being away from them. As an introvert, I admit that I recharge sometimes by spending time alone. But my time alone is with a book, or in prayer, or riding in the car to and from work.

You might ask, Isn't reading being isolated? I place reading in a different category because I am promoting before my children the excellent habit of reading. In addition, the books I choose to read boost my mental and spiritual growth. I read at least one book from nine different topic categories annually to develop myself as a Christian leader in the marketplace. I want my children to learn and grow continually, so I want them to see me modeling such behavior. The discipline of reading should be developed as a single man and carried over as a married man and father.

When we are with our families, we must be fully engaged with them. Playing board games at the kitchen table with your family is different from playing electronic games on the television by yourself. Joining the family in board games requires you to be with your loved ones and gives you the opportunity to build relationship capital with them.

I know you can play a video game with your son on the couch. However, the danger is that it leads both of you to play video games alone. I've never met anyone addicted to board games who then played them alone at the kitchen table. The same cannot be said about men described as gamers. These men spend too much time alone on the couch, and there are far too many of such men.

The overarching objective is not to be pleasure-seekers but disciplined sons of God who can teach discipline to our children, so that we all live holy and productive lives. But in closing, I want to repeat something I said earlier: pleasure, or having wholesome fun, is not wrong. It is part of our human experience and desire. It's undoubtedly a desire put into us by God Himself when He made mankind in His image. If you are a man with a family, however, pleasure should include your family members, like taking your wife out on a date, golfing with your sons, attending daddy-daughter dances with your girls, or simply participating in card games or board games with your kids. As family men, the goal should be to keep ourselves from pleasuring ourselves, by ourselves. This is the sin the Apostle John is talking about in 1 John, which Paul reiterates in his admonition for us to not gratify the desires of our sinful nature (Galatians 5:16).

Possessions

The second warning from John involves the lust of the eyes, which I described earlier as the desire for possessions. Men use their work as the justification for all kinds of selfish behavior, including the accumulation of possessions. We reward ourselves with the things of this world that we believe will bring us joy and pleasure. But he who dies with the most toys wins—nothing. Especially if we spent so much time at the office we neglected our families. We say noble things like working hard is for financing our children's education, or building a secure retirement, or buying a lake home to spend time with our grandchildren. When we talk and live this way, we act like the fool Jesus warned us about who did well on this earth, accumulating for himself great riches, but was poor in the things of God, which jeopardized his eternal soul (Luke 12:16–21).

Don't misunderstand me: having toys in this world is not sinful, nor is it sinful to enjoy them. The key is to focus on sharing them with our family and friends while enjoying life with them. Don't work so hard for possessions that you end up ignoring your loved ones today while you work to achieve some big future dream that you want to share with them tomorrow. They may not be interested in hanging out with you when tomorrow finally comes.

Promotions

The final warning in 1 John 2:16 concerns the pride of life—the unhealthy desire for success, the striving to be a somebody in this world. We use the desire to be leaders in our workplaces as an excuse to put in long hours so we can be promoted to the highest levels. This robs God and the people in our lives of our time, which is our greatest asset and the only one God forces us to use entirely every day.

Our true identity is not found in what we do or the titles we hold. Our identity is first and foremost as children of God, servants who have been assigned a mission from God: to see His Kingdom come and His will be done on earth as it is in heaven. Titles, treasures, and trophies will never replace the purpose for which God created us. A man of God protects himself from pursuing the things of this world so that he can protect his family from also pursuing worldly things. A man who is able to keep himself from pursuing worldly promotion is a man who can lead a church and a community into doing the right and good things that God requires, rather than pursue selfish and self-centered dead ends.

Prescriptions for Success Against the Flesh

God, in His word, provides us with some prescriptions for dealing with the weaknesses of our flesh. The first prescription—prayer—is found in Matthew 26:41, where Jesus recognizes Peter's desire to be strong when he is really weak. Jesus told Peter that the means for overcoming the weakness of the flesh was to pray for strength. As Jesus faced His greatest temptation there in the Garden of Gethsemane—to walk away from the Cross—He too prayed. His focus was not on failing God but on doing the will of God. When Jesus taught the disciples to pray in Matthew 6, He encouraged them to pray that they would not be led into temptation but delivered from evil. We are more easily led into temptation when we are idle and alone. Prayer takes us to God, and prayer for strength to do God's will keeps us focused on doing the work of God.

Ephesians 6:10–15 tells us to put on the whole armor of God. This is our second prescription for battling against the flesh. As biblical men, we not only armor-up to help us win our own battles with our flesh and this evil world, we also armor-up, if we are married men, for our family—for our sons but especially for our wives and daughters. A woman's primary spiritual protection is provided by her father when she is growing up, then her husband once she is married. We should be covering our wives and daughters in prayer and bathing them in the word, thus helping to equip them spiritually for living faithfully as daughters of God. Men are protectors and should stand in front of, not behind, those who are weaker. Even unbelieving men have espoused the principle of putting "women and children first" in times of danger. As biblical men we stand in front of our women and children when we stand before God for them in prayer. We further protect them by teaching them God's word and how to apply it so that they, too, will walk in God's ways just as we do. If you see yourself as the protector of your home and fully embrace this role and all it entails, you are less likely to indulge your flesh.

The Apostle Peter says the devil prowls around looking for someone to devour (1 Peter 5:8). It has often been said that the best defense is a good offense. We as biblical men are on offense when we are doing the will of God. When we do God's will, we cannot simultaneously sin against God. Therefore, keeping busy doing the will of God is the third prescription for winning the battle against our flesh. We are most vulnerable to being devoured by the devil when isolated, seeking our own selfish ends. We protect ourselves best when working in community with other believers to accomplish the purposes for which the Church has been left in this world (evangelism and service). We must resist temptation to keep the bad things out of our lives, but when they are gone we cannot leave our lives empty, we must also pursue the good things of the Christian life. Jesus said we were created to live abundant and full lives. We must have faith that abundant life is obtained when we pursue the purposes of God rather than the gratification of our flesh.

Following these three prescriptions—praying for strength, armoring-up and accepting our role as protectors of our families, and working diligently at doing God's will—can keep us from succumbing to the passivity and laziness of our flesh. We can successfully resist our fleshly desires for pleasure, possessions, and promotions when we replace those desires with prayer, a warrior mindset, and hands busy about the Father's business.

Living It Out: Personal Stories

I have not trained any of my children in combative fighting skills. I'm not opposed to this, but neither do I want to define protection as simply my ability to use my hands or a weapon to keep an enemy from harming me.

Most if not all of our need for protection will come in the necessity to keep ourselves from evil. Evil is rampant on the Internet and whatever device we allow ourselves to view. It also comes through the people we interact with who do not maintain their spiritual diligence as much as we do. This is why my wife and I have never allowed our children to participate in youth groups at church. These groups are essential ministries, but I believe they are most effective for children without Christian parents.

Christian parents should be responsible for discipling their children and not place that responsibility on others. If our children spend more time with their peers than they do with us, their peers will have a more significant influence on them, because they have a greater relationship with them. Our children's peers come from school, church, and the neighborhood your home is in. My goal for many years has been for no day, week, or month to go by in which my children spent more time with their peers than with their family. This was not an easy goal to achieve or maintain. It takes great vigilance on the part of the protective father, but influence is a product of relationship, and relationship is a product of time. Whoever accumulates the most time with our children will have the most significant influence on them. This is why we homeschool our children, so that we increase the time they have with their family instead of with their peers.

Do not be deceived; unfortunately, a typical Christian school or church youth group is filled with peers who do not know the Lord well. It's not the fault of the Christian school or the church per se; it's simply that the children in these organizations are still being discipled themselves and are not yet mature in the Lord; therefore, they are incapable of effectively discipling our children or positively influencing them. To put it another way, raising godly children will not happen by simply surrounding them with immature "godly" peers. I would suggest their peers are not godly, because they don't have enough maturity in Christ to be such, and therefore you and I as fathers must protect our children from their peers by limiting their time with them.

Much has already been written elsewhere about the dangers of cellphones, computers, and iPads in the hands of young people today. I won't belabor the point here. Still, I encourage you as a biblical man to take seriously your job as the protector of your home and keep a careful watch over these electronic intruders, which can quickly destroy your own life and the lives of your children if not diligently utilized for good.

A Manly Example

Job is my man of choice for exemplifying the life of a man who lived as a priest, provider, and protector. Job is one of the greatest heroes of the faith. In addition to the record we have of Job in the Old Testament book named for him, when God lists three great, righteous men in Ezekiel 14, Job is named among them. I chose Job for the following reasons.

Job served his family faithfully as a priest, offering sacrifices to God for even the possibility of his children sinning (Job 1:5). Job did all he could to ensure his children were right with God. Every father must instruct his children in God's ways, and petition God for mercy if his children stray from those ways.

As a protector, Job was faultless. I have already mentioned that biblical protection requires moral integrity. God says Job was blameless, upright, and shunned evil (Job 1:1). Job maintained his moral integrity despite Satan doing everything he could to harm him (except take his life, which God would not allow). Even when Job's wife invited him to curse God in his distress, Job refused (Job 2:9–10). Job protected his moral character no matter what.

Finally, Job was undoubtedly a great provider, as he was an immensely wealthy man (Job 1:3). Provision is more than big houses and nice clothes, and no excuse can be made for a man who pursues those things at the expense of his marriage or the spiritual loss of his children. Yet a man is responsible for housing, feeding, and clothing his wife and children, and Job was able to do so abundantly.

Job was a great man in the eyes of God and men because he was such a trustworthy man as a priest, provider, and protector. If we embrace these roles, we too will be honored by both God and man.

Chapter 4

Connecting to the Family of God

N—*A biblical man* **never** *is alone, but integrally connects himself to the family of God.*

One of the most neglected places in the heart of the Christian is love for the Church. Maybe I'm wrong about this, but the COVID pandemic and our responses to the ensuing lockdown have only furthered my conviction that I'm correct.

The Church is the bride of our Lord Jesus Christ. The Church is the body of Christ. He Himself is the head of this organization by which He makes visible His life on earth. Jesus plans to present the Church before His Father pure and undefiled. The man of God must love God's people; therefore, the man of God must love and be integrally connected to the Church of God.

There are at least three primary functions for men to perform within the Church. A biblical man is to *worship* with other believers, *encourage* those same believers, and *serve* with those believers.

Worshipping with Believers

So what does worship look like? First, a man must worship God in Spirit and in truth (John 4:23). What does this mean? Worshipping God in Spirit means being born again of the Spirit (John 3:5). We are not Christians because we go to church; we go to church because we are Christians. We become Christians when we confess our sins to Christ, because we understand we are sinners and want to repent before God of our sins. We ask Christ to forgive our sins, believing His death on the cross paid for our sins so that He can forgive our sins when we confess them to Him. Since Jesus died once for all sins, to be born again we need only repent once for our sins. While daily we confess our sins so that He might purify us from all unrighteousness (1 John 1:9), we are nevertheless permanently saved when we have one time wholeheartedly repented of and confessed our sins before Him.

Repentance means turning from one direction and heading in another direction. We not only confess our sins but also repent of our sins. That means we stop doing things that displease God and are committed to ending those things in our lives. Some of our sins are large and must be dealt with immediately, like stealing, adultery, fornication, drunkenness, etc. Other sins like impatience, selfishness, anger, and greed may take more time as the Spirit patiently does His work in us. Repentance means allowing and working with the Holy Spirit to accomplish His goal: our conformity to the very image of Jesus (Romans 8:29).

At some point the confession of our faith should be expressed publicly before the Church, symbolized by baptism. We must not be ashamed of Christ; rather, we must identify ourselves with Him. This public identification begins biblically by baptism and continues through our testimony every time we share with others what God has done in our lives. We should be able to easily articulate when, how, and why we came to faith in Jesus. There should be an identifiable time in our life when we recognized we were indeed sinners and needed forgiveness and, therefore, a Savior. If we cannot identify such a time, perhaps we truly have not been born again. Just as your mother can remember when you were born the first time, you should be able to identify when you were born again the second time.

I realize some of you were raised in Christian homes and struggle with identifying the specific moment of your rebirth. My children are in this camp. However, as I stressed with them, while in general they may have always been believers in Jesus as Savior, they needed to experience a moment of conviction when they realized that they themselves were sinners in need of that Savior. The Holy Spirit comes to convict the world of its sin, God's righteousness, and His coming judgment (John 16:8). Every believer should remember an encounter in their lives when the Holy Spirit convicted them of the unpleasant truth that they too were sinners who needed Jesus.

This conviction is what I believe it means to worship Jesus in truth. When we worship in truth, we recognize the reality that we are born sinful and unable by any human means to reconcile ourselves with God and must come to Jesus for reconciliation with the Father. We believe the truth found only in the Holy Bible: that Jesus is the Son of God, sent to the world by Father God to save the world; Jesus rose from the dead and will someday judge the world; Jesus will present His saved people to God to live forever with God; and Jesus as Savior is the only

One who can reconcile us to God, because He came from God to save sinners, which we all are before God. If we do not accept this truth, if we do not confess our sins before God and believe in our hearts that Jesus was raised from the dead to reconcile us to God, then we are not right with God. This results in not properly worshipping God in Spirit and in truth, which ultimately results in not living forever with God. We must be born again by the Spirit through believing the truth that God came to the world in Jesus and by confessing His Name in repentance, followed by allegiance to everything He commands us to do in the Scriptures (Matthew 28:20).

Many of you probably thought this worship section would be about singing songs to God in church on Sunday. That is praise, not worship. When Jesus spoke of true worshippers worshipping Him in Spirit and in truth, He was not referring to singing songs. Singing with other believers in church is great, because lifting our voices in praise is a byproduct of our love and devotion for the One True God. But it is not worship. Romans 12:1 describes true worship as presenting our bodies to God as a living sacrifice, holy and pleasing to Him. "Presenting our bodies" entails fully surrendering our minds and members to God's use and glory. Therefore, worship is not singing religious songs, though that is good. Worship is serving with the body of Christ to accomplish God's will on the earth.

Encouraging Believers

Because God is Father and we are His children, He commands we not give up meeting together but instead keep encouraging one another (Hebrews 10:24–25). This encouragement helps spur us on toward love and good deeds. Think of church as the huddle where we meet to learn the plays we are to execute throughout the week in our homes and workplaces. The "plays" we run each day reflect our commitment to God and doing His will, lived out through our loving actions and our testimonies about God to others. Initially, the Church met daily to encourage one another in this new life we have in Jesus (Acts 2:46). Far too many men make meeting with other believers just once a week an uphill task. This is not the image or example we want to give our children. Maybe church is not as fun for our kids as going to Grandpa's house; you may hear complaints from your kids that church is boring. Regardless, as biblical men we know that staying connected to the family of God is essential, and someday our children will, too, as long as we continue to model the important behavior of attending church faithfully.

The first mission of the Church is the Great Commission. In our Sunday "huddles" we should be spurring one another on in this mission of winning the lost in our spheres of influence. While we are not to use our workplaces simply as opportunities for evangelism, we are to evangelize at work whenever opportunities present themselves. We talk about every other subject under the sun at work. For the Christian, Jesus should be our most prevalent topic. Our shame of Jesus is why our culture is in chaos; few hear about Jesus from the Christians in their lives, so most are doing whatever is right in their own eyes. As we share Jesus in our homes, we become more comfortable talking about Him outside our homes. When we share with unbelievers at work and elsewhere about our life of faith, Peter warns us not to be obnoxious but gentle, and not to be afraid but to take every opportunity for sharing which presents itself (1 Peter 3:15). Our boss pays us to do a job that has nothing to do with evangelism, and we should strive do that job with excellence as working for the Lord

(Colossians 3:23). Excellent employees earn the respect of others and therefore may be more likely to be listened to when opportunities to interject spiritual topics present themselves. As workers for the Lord, we should be looking for ways to use our vocation to build His Kingdom on the earth as it is in heaven. We can encourage each other in this vital work when we meet with other believers in church.

We can't encourage other believers at church if we are not attending church. Some men avoid church when they feel they are not living like they should. One of the things guilt and shame does to us is isolate us. It's far easier to remain disconnected from the people of God than to connect to the people of God for our further spiritual development. Imagine the church as a gym and that we are all required by God to become physically fit. It is easier to avoid the gym and remain as we are than to go regularly to the gym and work hard to increase our strength, particularly when we see so many people at the gym that appear more fit than we are. Men shy away from hard work, accountability, and difficulty, but all of these things are important for developing not only physically but also spiritually. That is why, no matter how you might feel, as a biblical man you should keep attending church, where you can be encouraged and spurred on by other believers (Hebrews 10:24).

As with our family at home, our church family is where we meet people who are different from us and therefore sometimes agitate us. It is difficult to encourage other believers when we are miffed at them. As we read in Acts 6, in the earliest days of the Church conflict quickly arose between two different kinds of people within it: the Hellenistic Jews and the Hebraic Jews. Conflict is unavoidable in any family; we know that and experience that in our marriages with the people we love the most. So don't be discouraged when conflict happens in your church. Conflict can help make us all better Christians as we learn to compromise, reconcile, and love each other through it.

The purpose of the church is for us to be part of a fellowship that accomplishes more as we work together than we can through working alone. Jesus said all men would know that we are His disciples by our love for one another (John 13:35). In our fellowship, we demonstrate His life in us through working out our difficulties and working together to accomplish His mission.

Using the church-as-gym analogy again, it is when unbelievers see us in the gym with our various coaches encouraging us and moving us through our exercises, and they see us helping each other and growing stronger together, that they witness our good results and are attracted to our God.

The church is where we can break free from our isolation and loneliness. It is the fraternity we used to have or wish we had had growing up. Like family, church requires intentionality and hard work, but increasing the number of people in our lives who we love and who love us brings us the most profound pleasure. God made us for one another, even as He made us for Himself. God has always been in a relationship with Himself as the Father, the Son, and the Holy Spirit, and He made us for a relationship with Him and one another. We will never be complete until we are joined to our Christian brethren in purpose and fellowship, for encouragement and commitment, for accomplishment and development, until we all reach unity in the faith and full identity with Christ (Ephesians 4:13).

Therefore, men who are committed to God must be committed to their church and its mission. In general, the mission of any church is twofold: (1) to build up one another in Christ; and (2) to bring others into the family of God through sharing the gospel of Christ. A biblical man takes his place in the family to accomplish this mission. He finds where he can encourage and build up the body internally and join with others to grow the body externally. This means joining with those who study God's word, pray for God's Church, and serve God's people. It also means giving generously of our time, treasure, and talent to expand God's work in the communities where we live. The man of God puts his hand to the plow and doesn't look back (Luke 9:62). He is fully committed to the person of Jesus Christ, Who seeks laborers for His ripe harvest (Luke 10:2).

One of ways we can encourage other believers is to help them understand their gifting and place within the body. Frankly, not all churches do a good job of this. If your church falls into that category, you will have to work harder to find your particular place in the body of Christ. Seek out other believers who can help you understand your gifting and calling. They can encourage you and help you determine what God wants to accomplish through you. This is why it's so important for you to take your place in the fellowship of believers, especially a group of trusted men who can speak directly to you about what they see God working in you.

Some of the Bible's core teachings on this subject are found in Matthew 25:14–30, where Jesus indicates all of us are entrusted with natural talents bestowed by God, and in 1 Corinthians chapters 12–14, where the Apostle Paul explains that each one of us has been equipped by the Spirit with spiritual gifts for serving His Church. God saves us for good works, specific works He had in mind when He created us (Ephesians 2:10). These natural and supernatural talents are to be used to build God's Kingdom through evangelism and discipleship. As biblical men we are to take our place among the family of believers and use our talents to make the family grow, and nurture and encourage its members.

Spiritual gifts are not natural to us but are given to us by the Holy Spirit at the point of need for accomplishing His work. Most of us are unfamiliar with spiritual gifts because we rely too heavily on our natural talents and therefore accomplish too little for the Kingdom. Spiritual gifts are part of God's supernatural presence in our lives. These gifts are not about us and cannot be manufactured by us; they come from God, the Spirit, Who gives when He wills, how He wills, and to whom He wills. But we are to seek spiritual gifts earnestly because they help us encourage other believers and in other ways serve our church. They also enable nonbelievers to see God in us more clearly, which helps them come to know Jesus as Savior and Lord.

Living It Out: Personal Stories

As a homeschool father who made it his goal to have more time invested in the life of my children than any other person or group, the constant pushback I received from my children was the lack of friends they had in their lives. This pushback did not bother me because, based on my experience, I know that childhood friends are not that important; I only have one childhood friend still actively in my life today. (Though admittedly, many of my old school chums are now “friends” with me again on Facebook. For this I am thankful, because Facebook has allowed me to share Christ with them through social media.) Likewise, my college buddies are at best loose acquaintances of mine now. My current best friends are those from my church who are on the same mission as I am for raising godly kids and winning the lost to Christ. My children have not accumulated the personal history to understand this common human experience—that childhood and college friends typically don’t last and are therefore not crucially important—so they desire to have more friends today. My belief that time spent together determines the depth of the relationship, which determines the degree of influence, has driven my actions to limit my children's time with their peers. So what do I do to provide my children with a healthy social life?

First, our family attends church together, and we look for areas there to serve. This has meant serving during festivals and holidays with our church. It has also meant serving during various church projects and ministry opportunities, including short-term mission trips. We are part of a church small group that is family-integrated; that is, in our small group we don't separate our children from the adults during our discussion time. Admittedly, over the years this has become increasingly harder to do, because many parents today are not discipling their children effectively.

My children also work with other families in a weekly outreach to local inner-city elementary schools. For nearly 20 years, we have been able to conduct a vacation bible school–type curriculum as a unique after-school program in various elementary schools in our area. This has allowed my children to do ministry with their Christian peers, providing them with social interaction with others their age while significantly growing their faith. I have loved how much of a positive impact this after-school ministry has had on my children's lives.

Christians must be part of the body of Christ, so my wife and I have sought to model for our children the importance of weekly worship, participation in Bible and other studies, and serving the church and the community as a family. All these activities have provided social outlets for my children.

As a biblical man, you should prioritize the family of God for your children over the gods of this age: sports, dance, and music. Too many men allow their children to play sports on Sunday at the cost of participating in church. Most of these children do not become professional athletes but do become poor Christians. Even if our children did become professional athletes, what good is it for them to gain the world but forfeit their souls? Time together with the family of God serving the Lord will have a tremendous impact on your children's spiritual development, a result that participation in sports rarely, if ever, achieves. Also, interacting with others in the household of God takes the pressure off you to be the "perfect" Christian man and father. I am not that perfect man; I suspect that neither are you. Therefore, we need the body of Christ to help fill the gaps in areas where we fall short. But to benefit from the body of Christ we must spend time with the body of Christ, participating with them in the things of the Lord. This benefits us as well as our children.

Serving with Believers

Another way to utilize our talents and gifts and connect to the family of God is by serving. The opportunities to serve our church and the world at large are numerous, for, as Jesus said, the laborers are few. A biblical man participates in the various opportunities his church has to serve the body and grow the body. As he takes advantage of these opportunities, he will discover what he is passionate about, and the work God made him specifically to accomplish. As just mentioned, Ephesians 2:10 clearly states that God created us with works in mind that He wants to accomplish through us, which we must discover through perseverance, prayer, and participation in the body of Christ. It would be nice if God would just send us an email telling us specifically what He wants us to do, but He doesn't. Instead, He enjoys helping us discover and understand what we are to do, because in this process we are made stronger and better for accomplishing the works He has given us.

In serving God with His people, we discover where our talents can be best utilized and position ourselves for His Spirit to accomplish through us what only He can do. Faith is exercised when we go beyond our comfort zone to obey God. Without faith, it is impossible to please God (Hebrews 11:6). We please God when we obey Him even though it stretches us beyond our current capacities and we must call on Him to provide His power and presence to accomplish His will. When we live for God's glory by faith, we will experience His presence and know His joy, for He takes great delight in the man who obeys and trusts Him.

Being integrally connected to the family of God means participating in our church and committing ourselves to it, where we build the Kingdom of God with the people of God to the glory of God. That is what biblical men do; they commit and participate with God's people in accomplishing God's purposes. A man of God must be involved in the Church of God, for that is the will of God for every man who claims to be a son of God.

A Manly Example

Barnabas is depicted in the New Testament as a godly man who gave his treasure to the people of God, gave his time to building relationships within the family of God, and gave his talents to building the Kingdom of God. This great man of God is mentioned over 30 times in the Bible.

Barnabas is introduced to us in the fourth chapter of Acts as a Levite, a religious leader whose name originally was Joseph. Right away we see he is all-in for the Kingdom. This greatly encourages the apostles, who see a ripe harvest but few laborers. So the apostles call him Barnabas, which means "son of encouragement." His first encouraging act was to sell some property and give the proceeds to the church to meet its needs. Giving is fundamental to the Christian life. As biblical men we should be marked by generosity, even as God gives to us so generously. Our children should describe us as generous, for this is foundational to the character of God, Who they are experiencing through us as fathers.

Our next biblical encounter with Barnabas is after the conversion of the Apostle Paul (Acts 9). Saul, the previous name for Paul, was so antagonistic to the church that the church feared accepting him upon his conversion. The son of encouragement, Barnabas, placed his reputation on the line by bringing Paul to the church leaders and vouching for his legitimacy. The Lord blesses a peacemaker; Jesus said that our most powerful testimony to the world would be our love for one another (John 13:35). Barnabas helped the early church greatly by making peace between Jesus' apostles in Jerusalem and Jesus' greatest missionary apostle.

In Acts 11, Barnabas is described as a good man, full of the Holy Spirit and strong in faith. Along with Paul, he stays in Antioch for a year, teaching large crowds of people about Jesus. Barnabas is an encourager, a joiner, and a connector who sees needs and puts people in place to meet those needs. In Acts 15, his love for others would result in his breaking his partnership with the great Apostle Paul. Unlike Paul, Barnabas would not discard Mark, who disengaged from Paul and Barnabas in a previous mission. Barnabas's insistence that Mark was worthy of a second chance caused a rift between Barnabas and Paul but would later result in Paul and Mark being reconciled in ministry (2 Timothy 4:11). We assume that Paul and Barnabas must have reconciled as well, though the Scripture doesn't say so explicitly.

Finally, the book of Acts fills in the rest of its description of Barnabas by recording his missionary journeys with Paul (Acts 14–15). Paul reiterates this missionary work in his letters to the Corinthians, Galatians, and Colossians.

Barnabas was a faithful companion of a great man of God. Barnabas also served the work of God in his capacity as a reconciler, encourager, and missionary. We may not have Barnabas's giftings, but, like him, we can certainly do all we can to give generously, live at peace with our brothers, and bring as many people as possible into the Kingdom of God by faithfully sharing the gospel.

Chapter 5

What's Next?

I hope you found this book encouraging and practical for becoming a biblical man and, if you are a father, raising your sons to be real men and teaching your daughters how to recognize real men. The world today is in desperate need of biblical men.

So what's the next step? Go through the three attributes of a biblical man, assessing how you and your son(s) are doing with these attributes:

- **M**akes loving God and doing His will first priority
- **A**ccepts responsibility for himself and his family as priest, provider, and protector
- **N**ever is alone, but integrally connects himself to the family of God

Consider what it means to make loving God and doing his will your first priority. Our love for someone is expressed by our time with someone. Therefore, if we are not consistently reading the Bible and praying to its Author, that is the first place to begin. We must be consistent readers and students of the Scriptures. We can't go anywhere else with God before we fuel ourselves with His presence daily through His word. As mentioned in Chapter 2, there are many free Bible reading plans online; for example, you can find a simple reading plan on my website at www.knowGodcoach.com.

Accepting responsibility for yourself and your family as priest, provider, and protector applies what you're learning from step one to your family as step two. Accepting responsibility for yourself also means committing to growing your faith through your church with a band of brothers. Meet consistently with godly men to pray and study God's word. If you don't have a group that you can join, take the initiative and start a group. It's no more complicated than asking one or two men to join you in weekly prayer and Bible reading to talk about what God's word says and how you can apply it to your lives.

Being a biblical man means working and providing for yourself and your family. So if you don't have a job, get one. If your wife is the primary breadwinner, think about that seriously and what you can do about it.

If you are allowing trash in your life, stop it. Protect yourself from pornography and covetousness. If you are reading or watching things that feed this beast, kill it. You might even have to get a new job if you're overwhelmed by temptations where you work. Whatever it takes to protect yourself from evil, do it! One means of protecting yourself (and by extension, your family) is joining a band of brothers who can strengthen you as you in turn strengthen them to renounce this broken world and its ways.

Finally, connect to a church if you haven't already, then—I'm saying it again because it is so important—connect to a group of men who love the Lord and want to please Him just as you do. I hope you are getting the point that trying to be a biblical man as a Lone Ranger does not work! Get into a church where the Bible is taught and elevated as the chief source for knowing God's will. Get around some men who love God and want to obey His commands. Be that man yourself. Talk about what you're learning from the Scriptures with other men and ask them what they are learning. Read books that strengthen your faith and discuss them with other men who are also reading to grow in faith. Pray with men. Pray as often as you can with other men. The prayers of a righteous man avail much (James 5:16).

The Christian faith is not about just knowing God's word; it's *doing* God's word. Find some Christian brothers and begin serving God together. Serve the discouraged, the addicted, the elderly, the widows, the single parents, and the divorced in your church. Serve in some capacity in your community. Serving is fundamental to being a Christian. Jesus did not come to be served but to serve (Matthew 20:28).

Share your faith with others. This is critical for true discipleship and advances the main purpose for the Church remaining on the earth. The Great Commission is the mission of every Christian. What are you doing to see God's Kingdom grow in breadth (evangelism) and depth (discipleship) where He planted you? What can you do to bear more fruit? Fruit that will last, the true mark of a follower of Jesus (John 15:16). It takes a real man to identify himself with Jesus in today's culture. You have to have backbone, courage, and guts. You don't have to be obnoxious or rude, just unashamed of Jesus and passionate to do what you can to keep everyone you know who doesn't know Jesus from spending their eternity in hell.

Read this book with your sons. Read this book with your sons-in-law. Confess your sins to one another and resolve to improve together. Read this book with some men from your church. Again, confess with them where you have failed, vow to improve, and pray for one another to become strong men of God at home and in your community.

Becoming a biblical man is simple but not easy. You can do it, but you have to decide to do it. A biblical man is not passive. A biblical man takes action to move toward the things of God to do the will of God, so that he glorifies God and receives His reward on that day when he meets God face to face.

As I was wrapping up the writing of this book, I was riding in the car one day with two of my sons, taking an opportunity to further define manhood for them. I was chastising one of my sons because his slowness to get in the car meant we might be late for the appointment we were scheduled to attend. I told him men honor their commitments: men plan, prepare, and execute. This is required of men, for it is required of leaders. This is what you must do if you are going to be successful at raising godly men and giving your daughters in marriage to godly men. You must plan to raise biblical men, prepare them for manhood, and execute your plan, adjusting it along the way as necessary but sticking to it.

This book gives you a plan. But preparing yourself and your family to know God, do His will, and participate in His Church is up to you. You must execute the plan. You must build relational capital with your sons and daughters—a product of time—to influence their lives. Lead them to where you want them to go. If you lead them to where they are supposed to go, they will not depart from that way when they are older (Proverbs 22:6). Where are they supposed to go? Toward Jesus, and obedience to everything He teaches. This is the way all of us are supposed to go.

I have given you a target: biblical manhood. You must pray and think about how you will help your son(s) hit that target, even as you model moving toward that target yourself. You must have a good relationship with your children if you are going to guide them toward the target. The person with the most time equity in your children will have the most influence on your children. If you allow school, church youth groups, and neighborhood kids to occupy most of your children's time, your children's peers will influence them the most, with sometimes disastrous results. If you occupy your children's time the most, you will have the most influence on them.

This is why my wife and I chose to homeschool our children, so we could spend lots of time with them and be the dominating influence in their lives. All ten of my children walk with the Lord as of this writing. First and foremost, that's due to the grace of God. But I believe it is also due in part to the time we put into our children—instructing them, modeling behaviors, and leading them in the way they should go. Of course, there is much more to say about raising children, but that is beyond the scope of this book. For now, suffice it to say that as a biblical man you must plan, prepare, then execute your plan with full intentionality and effort if you want to raise children who will live forever with you in the Kingdom of God.

I opened this book quoting King David's charge to his son Solomon to "be a man." I hope I have accomplished the mission of more clearly defining what David meant by that vague phrase. Let me conclude by echoing that charge again, but this time from the Apostle Paul. In 1 Corinthians 16:13 (ESV), Paul states: "Be watchful, stand firm in the faith, act like men, be strong." A biblical man makes knowing God and doing His will his first priority. He accepts responsibility for himself and his family as priest, provider, and protector. A biblical man does not do life alone, but integrally connects himself to the family of God.

You can do it! If you'd like, I would be happy to help you by coming to your church and assisting you with launching a men's group committed to developing biblical men. Whatever it takes, let's do it! Let us live like men!

Made in United States
North Haven, CT
19 February 2023

32865027R00065